AF316683

THE ETHICS OF EMPATHY

A JOURNEY TOWARD COMPASSIONATE LIVING

DR. MINAKSHI BANSAL

Made with ♥ on the Notion Press Platform
www.notionpress.com

DEDICATION

Dedicated to all those who believe in the
transformative power of empathy, and to those who
strive to cultivate compassion and understanding in
every interaction. May our collective journey
toward a more empathetic world be filled with
grace, resilience, and profound moments of
connection.

ppp

Contents

Contents

Prayer

"Om Bhadram Karnebhih Shrinuyama Devah
Bhadram Pashyemakshabhiryajatrah
Sthirairangais Tushtuvamsastanubhih
Vyashema Devahitam Yadayuh
Svasti Na Indro Vriddhashravah
Svasti Nah Pusha Vishwavedah
Svasti Nastarkshyo Arishtanemih
Svasti No Brihaspatir Dadhatu
Om Shantih Shantih Shantih"

This mantra is a prayer for universal well-being, invoking the blessings of various deities for protection, health, and happiness. It emphasizes the importance of experiencing the auspicious through all senses and living a life aligned with divine purpose. The repetition of "Shantih" at the end signifies a deep desire for peace in the individual, the environment, and the universe at large. This mantra is often recited as a prayer for peace, prosperity, and the physical and spiritual well-being of all beings.

ᐅᐅᐅ

About The Author

Dr. Minakshi Bansal, born in the bustling metropolis of Delhi, India, has led a life steeped in artistry, scholarly pursuit, and an unwavering commitment to societal betterment. Following her marriage, she relocated to Ahmedabad, Gujarat, where she has since blossomed into a multifaceted beacon of inspiration for many. Dr. Minakshi is not only recognized as a gifted artist in the realm of Fine Arts but also as an esteemed author, a devoted social worker and a dedicated research scholar in Psychology. Her journey, marked by a profound dedication to elevating those around her, especially the downtrodden and underprivileged children of society, is a testament to her deep-seated belief in the transformative power of engagement and empathy.

From her earliest days, Minakshi was distinguished by an insatiable appetite for reading. Her literary universe was inhabited by characters and narratives that spanned ethical tales, motivational and inspirational stories, and the mythic parables imbued with life lessons. This voracious reading habit was not merely for personal edification but was driven by a desire to distill and disseminate the essence of these narratives to foster the development of students and peers alike. She was particularly captivated by the lives and teachings of historical figures and spiritual leaders such as Adi Shankaracharya, Swami Vivekananda, Dr. APJ Abdul Kalam, Mahamana Pandit Madan Mohan Malviya, Mahatma Gandhi, Sardar Vallabhai Patel, and Vinoba Bhave, among others. Their philosophies and life stories fueled her ambition to embody their ideals of resilience, selflessness, and relentless pursuit of knowledge.

Dr. Minakshi's academic and practical engagement with psychology has been equally noteworthy. As a research scholar, her focus has been on exploring the intricate tapestry of the human psyche, aiming to unlock the potential for psychological well-being and societal harmony. Her scholarly work is complemented by her active involvement in social work, where she employs her academic insights to make tangible differences in the lives of the underprivileged. Her endeavours in social work are characterized by an innovative approach that combines traditional wisdom with contemporary psychological practices to address the multifaceted challenges faced by these communities.

Her artistic talents, another facet of her diverse capabilities, are not merely a personal passion but also serve as a medium through which she communicates and connects with others. Her art, rich in symbolism and emotional depth, reflects her philosophical inquiries and social concerns, offering viewers a glimpse into the breadth of her intellect and the depth of her compassion.

In addition to her contributions to the arts and social sciences, Dr. Minakshi has embraced the healing arts of Pranic Healing, mastering the techniques developed by Master Choa Kok Sui. This practice, which focuses on the manipulation of Prana or life energy to heal the body and aura, has been both a personal journey of discovery and a means through which she extends her healing touch to others. Her proficiency in Pranic Healing is complemented by her advocacy and teaching of various forms of meditation aimed at rejuvenation, personal betterment, and the cultivation of harmony within individuals and communities alike.

Dr. Minakshi's life is a narrative of relentless pursuit, not just of personal achievement but of the upliftment and empowerment of society at large. Her diverse interests and talents—spanning the arts, literature, psychology, and the healing practices—converge on a singular path of service. She embodies the spirit of the luminaries who inspired her, channelling their legacy through her actions and teachings. Through her books, art, and social initiatives, she continues to inspire a new generation to embark on their own journeys of self-discovery, resilience, and altruism.

Her commitment to social betterment, particularly her focus on uplifting underprivileged children, reflects a deep understanding of the transformative potential of education and personal development. By integrating her knowledge of psychology, her artistic sensibilities, and her healing practices, Dr. Bansal has developed a holistic approach to social work that addresses both the immediate needs and the long-term well-being of the communities she serves.

As an author, Dr. Minakshi's writings offer a blend of inspirational insights, practical wisdom, and reflective contemplations drawn from her extensive reading and life experiences. Her books serve as a guide for those seeking to navigate the complexities of life with grace, resilience, and purpose. Through her narratives, she extends an invitation to her readers to explore the depths of their own potential and to contribute meaningfully to the collective well-being of society.

In Dr. Minakshi Bansal, we find a remarkable synthesis of the artist, the scholar, the healer, and the social activist. Her life's work stands as a beacon of hope and a source of inspiration for individuals seeking to make a difference in the world. Her story is a compelling reminder of the power of individual action, rooted in compassion and driven by a profound commitment to the betterment of humanity. Dr. Minakshi's legacy is not just in the tangible outcomes of her efforts but in the enduring spirit of inquiry, empathy, and service that she embodies.

ᏏᏏᏏ

Preface

In an age characterized by rapid technological advancement and global connectivity, the need for a deeper understanding of each other's experiences and challenges has never been more pronounced. As societies become increasingly diverse and complex, the call for a greater capacity for empathy emerges as a central theme in discussions ranging from interpersonal relationships to international diplomacy. This book is born out of the conviction that nurturing empathy is not just a moral imperative but a practical necessity in today's world.

Throughout this book, I explore the multifaceted nature of empathy, dissecting its various dimensions and the roles it plays across different spheres of life. From personal relationships and workplace environments to broader societal interactions, empathy has the power to transform lives and communities. By examining empathy through a multitude of lenses—psychological, social, cultural, and ethical—this book aims to illuminate the pathways through which we can enhance our ability to understand and connect with others.

The journey of writing this book began with a series of questions: What does it truly mean to empathize with another? How can we cultivate a more empathetic society? What are the barriers that prevent us from empathizing with others, and how can we overcome them? These questions led to years of research, interviews, and personal reflections, the synthesis of which is presented in these chapters.

Each chapter of the book delves into a different aspect of empathy. From its neurological underpinnings to its expression in literature and art, from its impact on leadership to its critical role in healthcare, the discussions are designed to provide a comprehensive overview of empathy's applications and benefits.

The exploration is not just academic; it is intensely practical, offering readers actionable insights and strategies to enhance their empathetic capacities.

A significant part of the book is dedicated to addressing the challenges of empathy. It is important to recognize that empathy is not a panacea; it has its limitations and can, if misapplied, lead to burnout or emotional fatigue. This book discusses these darker aspects of empathy and offers guidance on how to manage and mitigate them effectively. The balance between engaging empathetically and maintaining one's emotional health is delicate but crucial, and the book provides tools to navigate this balance.

Furthermore, the book examines the global implications of empathy. In an interconnected world, the ripple effects of empathy can extend far beyond individual interactions. Empathy has the potential to influence global policies and initiatives, impacting issues such as climate change, international conflicts, and global pandemics. This book discusses how cultivating empathy on a global scale can lead to more sustainable and peaceful solutions to worldwide challenges.

In addition to theoretical discussions, this book is rich with real-life examples, case studies, and personal stories that bring the concepts of empathy to life. These stories not only illustrate the power of empathy but also highlight the diverse ways in which it manifests in different contexts and cultures. They serve as a testament to the universal relevance of empathy and its capacity to enrich human lives.

The writing of this book has been a transformative journey, not just for me as an author but for everyone involved. It has been a process of discovery, learning, and, most importantly, reflection. The insights gathered from various experts, the heartfelt stories shared by individuals from all walks of life, and the latest research findings have all contributed to a rich tapestry of knowledge that underscores the importance of empathy.

As you embark on reading this book, I invite you to reflect on your own experiences with empathy. Consider the ways in which empathy has influenced your relationships, your work, and your understanding of the world. It is my hope that this book will not only provide you with a deeper insight into the nature of empathy but will also inspire you to cultivate it more consciously in every aspect of your life.

This book is an invitation—an invitation to journey toward more compassionate living through the practice of empathy. Whether you are a professional looking to enhance empathy in your practice, a parent aiming to instill empathetic values in your children, or simply a person interested in living a more connected and fulfilling life, this book offers valuable insights and practical advice to help you on your way.

ᗷᗷᗷ

ONE

UNDERSTANDING EMPATHY: THE HEART OF COMPASSION

Empathy is often considered the emotional and cognitive ability to step into the shoes of another person, to understand their feelings, and to see things from their perspective. This capacity for empathy not only involves feeling what another person feels but also entails a certain level of detachment to offer appropriate emotional or practical support. It is this dual nature—emotional resonance and thoughtful response—that makes empathy a cornerstone of compassionate living.

The Components of Empathy

Empathy comprises several components, each contributing uniquely to how we connect with others. Cognitive empathy, for example, is the ability to understand another person's thoughts and emotions intellectually. It allows us to comprehend the reasons behind people's feelings and behaviors without necessarily sharing those emotions. Emotional empathy, on the other hand, is about sharing the emotional experience of others, feeling what they feel as though their emotions were contagious. This emotional sharing can help forge deep personal connections but requires regulation to avoid emotional overwhelm. Another aspect, compassionate empathy, combines understanding and feeling with a motivation to act, to alleviate the suffering of others.

The Benefits of Empathy

Empathetic individuals tend to have richer social interactions and more satisfying personal relationships. Empathy promotes deeper bonding and reduces conflicts by enhancing understanding and tolerance among individuals. In professional settings, empathy contributes to better teamwork and leadership, as it enables leaders and team members to address concerns and motivate individuals effectively. In broader societal contexts, empathy fosters social harmony and aids in conflict resolution, as it promotes a deeper understanding of diverse perspectives and life experiences.

Empathy and Moral Judgment

Empathy extends beyond mere emotion and plays a crucial role in ethical decision-making. It helps individuals navigate complex moral landscapes by considering the impacts of actions on others, leading to more conscientious and ethical choices. By putting ourselves in someone else's position, we are more likely to act in ways that are considerate and just, reducing harm and enhancing benefits for others.

Cultivating Empathy

Despite its natural presence in human behavior, empathy is also a skill that can be cultivated and strengthened through practice. Techniques such as active listening, where one gives full attention to the speaker without planning a response, help enhance empathetic understanding. Engaging with diverse groups and exposing oneself to various life experiences can also broaden one's empathetic range by familiarizing oneself with different ways of living and perspectives.

Challenges to Empathy

However, empathy is not without its challenges. Factors like personal bias, cultural differences, and emotional fatigue can hinder empathetic engagement. Sometimes, too much empathy can lead to emotional burnout, particularly in professions involving constant caregiving. Therefore, learning to manage one's empathetic engagements—knowing when to step back and replenish one's emotional reserves—is crucial for maintaining effective and healthy empathy.

Empathy is the essence of human connection and a fundamental part of living compassionately. It allows us to understand and share the feelings of others, to offer help, and to make ethical decisions that consider the well-being of others. As we navigate our lives and interactions, cultivating a balanced approach to empathy can lead to more meaningful relationships and a more compassionate society.

❧❧❧

"Empathy is the language of the heart, spoken
fluently by those who listen with compassion,
understand without judgment, and act with
kindness."

♡♡♡

TWO

THE SCIENCE OF FEELING: HOW EMPATHY WORKS IN THE BRAIN

Empathy is not merely a social or emotional phenomenon; it is deeply rooted in the neurobiological processes of the brain. Recent advances in neuroscience have begun to unveil the complex brain networks that enable individuals to understand and share the feelings of others. These insights are critical not only for understanding how empathy works but also for addressing conditions where empathy is impaired.

Brain Regions Involved in Empathy

Empathy involves several key areas of the brain, each playing a distinct role in processing the different aspects of empathetic experience. The prefrontal cortex is crucial for cognitive empathy, which involves understanding the mental states of others. This area of the brain helps us to reason about others' thoughts and predict their reactions.

The amygdala, known for its role in emotional processing, is vital for emotional empathy. It responds to the emotional stimuli of others, triggering corresponding emotional reactions in ourselves.

Another significant area is the anterior insula, which is involved in the subjective experience of emotions. This region helps us to physically feel what another person is feeling as if those emotions were our own, a phenomenon often referred to as affective sharing.

The mirror neuron system, which includes regions like the inferior frontal gyrus and the inferior parietal lobule, also plays a role in empathy. These neurons activate both when a person performs an action and when they observe the same action performed by another, thus supporting the mimetic components of empathy.

How Empathy Is Processed

Empathy is processed through complex interactions between these brain regions. When we observe someone in pain, for instance, the neural circuits that are activated in our brains are remarkably similar to those activated if we were experiencing the pain ourselves. This neural mirroring is a fundamental mechanism by which empathy occurs.

However, empathy is more than just automatic neural responses; it also involves top-down processes such as emotional regulation and perspective-taking. The medial prefrontal cortex plays a crucial role in these aspects, helping us to not only share feelings but also regulate them and maintain an appropriate emotional distance. This balance ensures that we empathize effectively without becoming overwhelmed by others' emotional states.

The Role of Neurotransmitters and Hormones

Neurotransmitters and hormones also significantly influence empathy. Oxytocin, often dubbed the "love hormone," is particularly important. Research has shown that oxytocin can enhance the ability to read others' emotions and increase feelings of closeness and bonding. Dopamine, another critical neurotransmitter, is linked to the reward system in the brain and is associated with the pleasurable aspects of social interactions, potentially incentivizing empathetic behaviors.

Genetic and Environmental Influences on Empathy

Empathy is also shaped by a combination of genetic factors and environmental influences. Genetic predispositions can affect how brain structures related to empathy are formed and how they function. Meanwhile, environmental factors—such as upbringing, culture, and education—play a significant role in shaping how empathy is expressed and applied. Positive social interactions and environments that encourage emotional expression and understanding can enhance empathetic abilities.

Empathy in Clinical Contexts

Understanding the brain basis of empathy has profound implications for clinical practice, particularly in treating disorders characterized by empathy deficits, such as autism spectrum disorders, schizophrenia, and certain personality disorders.

Therapeutic strategies aimed at enhancing empathy could involve behavioral interventions, pharmacological approaches targeting neurotransmitter systems, or novel methods like neurofeedback, which trains individuals to regulate their brain activity.

The neuroscience of empathy not only deepens our understanding of what it means to connect with others but also opens up pathways for promoting more empathetic societies. By exploring how empathy works in the brain, we can better address the psychological and neurobiological barriers to empathy and harness its full potential for improving human relationships and well-being.

❦❦❦

"In a world where differences divide, empathy
becomes the bridge that connects souls,
transcending barriers of culture, language, and
belief."

♡♡♡

THREE

HISTORICAL PERSPECTIVES ON EMPATHY AND ETHICS

Empathy, as a concept, has roots that extend deep into human history, influencing ethical systems across various cultures and epochs. In ancient philosophical traditions, empathy—or the moral imperative to recognize and respond to the emotional states of others—was often encapsulated in the principle of treating others as one would wish to be treated.

In ancient Greece, philosophers like Aristotle spoke of empathy in terms of "sympatheia," a concept that captures a community of feelings among individuals. Aristotle's theory of ethics emphasized the importance of emotional attunement to others' experiences as a cornerstone of virtue and moral character. His notion of "phronesis" or practical wisdom, involved an empathetic understanding of others' situations, informing ethical decision-making and fostering communal bonds.

Similarly, in ancient Eastern philosophies, such as those found in India and China, empathy was integral to ethical thinking. The Indian spiritual texts like the Upanishads highlight the idea of seeing oneself in others and others in oneself, promoting a form of universal empathy that transcends individual ego. In Confucianism, the concept of "ren" or benevolence denotes an empathetic concern for others, encouraging individuals to act with kindness and understanding towards all.

Empathy in Medieval and Renaissance Thought

Moving into the medieval period, Christian theologians such as Thomas Aquinas incorporated Aristotelian philosophy into their ethics, interpreting empathy within the framework of charity and compassion. Aquinas argued that true compassion, driven by love, involves a shared emotional response to another's suffering, which then motivates moral actions.

During the Renaissance, the revival of classical texts brought renewed interest in humanistic approaches to empathy. Thinkers like Erasmus and Montaigne celebrated the capacity for humans to connect with and understand others' emotional states, arguing that this understanding was crucial for moral and civil society. Montaigne, in his essays, explored the idea of empathy as a way to bridge cultural and individual differences, promoting tolerance and a shared sense of humanity.

The Enlightenment and the Moral Sense Theory

The Enlightenment era brought a more systematic exploration of empathy, particularly through the moral sense theory advanced by philosophers such as David Hume and Adam Smith. Hume argued that humans naturally possess a "fellow-feeling" that is essential for moral judgment. According to Hume, our ability to empathize with others' joy or suffering directly influences our moral decisions.

Adam Smith, often known for his economic theories, also delved deeply into the role of empathy in ethics. In his theory, the "impartial spectator" process involves stepping into another's shoes and judging our own and others' actions from an empathetic standpoint. Smith posited that this capacity for empathy underpins all human interactions and is fundamental to the social fabric.

Nineteenth and Twentieth Century Developments

In the nineteenth century, empathy started to be studied not just philosophically but also psychologically. The German philosopher Theodor Lipps introduced the concept of "Einfühlung" (literally, "feeling into"), which later translated into the English word "empathy." Lipps' theory suggested that aesthetic appreciation involved projecting one's own emotional state onto objects and works of art, thereby extending the scope of empathy beyond interpersonal relationships.

The 20th century saw further expansion in the study of empathy, influenced by psychological and neuroscientific discoveries. The development of psychological theories like those of Carl Rogers emphasized empathy as a core component of effective psychotherapy, promoting an understanding that goes beyond cognitive awareness to a deep, affective sharing of experiences.

Contemporary Perspectives and Challenges

Today, the discussion of empathy continues to evolve, particularly as global connectivity and social media change the ways in which we interact with and understand others. Current ethical discussions around empathy also face challenges related to empathy fatigue, the ethics of care, and the implications of empathetic biases.

Empathy's journey through history reveals its integral role in shaping ethical thought and human relationships. By understanding its historical development, we can appreciate the complexity of empathy and its enduring importance in promoting ethical behavior and mutual understanding across different cultures and societies. This historical perspective not only enriches our understanding of empathy but also highlights its potential to foster a more compassionate and ethical world.

ϷϷϷ

"The true measure of our humanity lies not in our accomplishments but in our capacity to empathize—to feel deeply, connect genuinely, and uplift each other with empathy's gentle touch."

❦❦❦

FOUR

EMPATHY IN EVERYDAY LIFE: PRACTICAL APPLICATIONS

Empathy, as a concept, has roots that extend deep into human history, influencing ethical systems across various cultures and epochs. In ancient philosophical traditions, empathy—or the moral imperative to recognize and respond to the emotional states of others—was often encapsulated in the principle of treating others as one would wish to be treated.

In ancient Greece, philosophers like Aristotle spoke of empathy in terms of "sympatheia," a concept that captures a community of feelings among individuals. Aristotle's theory of ethics emphasized the importance of emotional attunement to others' experiences as a cornerstone of virtue and moral character. His notion of "phronesis" or practical wisdom, involved an empathetic understanding of others' situations, informing ethical decision-making and fostering communal bonds.

Similarly, in ancient Eastern philosophies, such as those found in India and China, empathy was integral to ethical thinking. The Indian spiritual texts like the Upanishads highlight the idea of seeing oneself in others and others in oneself, promoting a form of universal empathy that transcends individual ego. In Confucianism, the concept of "ren" or benevolence denotes an empathetic concern for others, encouraging individuals to act with kindness and understanding towards all.

Empathy in Medieval and Renaissance Thought

Moving into the medieval period, Christian theologians such as Thomas Aquinas incorporated Aristotelian philosophy into their ethics, interpreting empathy within the framework of charity and compassion. Aquinas argued that true compassion, driven by love, involves a shared emotional response to another's suffering, which then motivates moral actions.

During the Renaissance, the revival of classical texts brought renewed interest in humanistic approaches to empathy. Thinkers like Erasmus and Montaigne celebrated the capacity for humans to connect with and understand others' emotional states, arguing that this understanding was crucial for moral and civil society. Montaigne, in his essays, explored the idea of empathy as a way to bridge cultural and individual differences, promoting tolerance and a shared sense of humanity.

The Enlightenment and the Moral Sense Theory

The Enlightenment era brought a more systematic exploration of empathy, particularly through the moral sense theory advanced by philosophers such as David Hume and Adam Smith. Hume argued that humans naturally possess a "fellow-feeling" that is essential for moral judgment. According to Hume, our ability to empathize with others' joy or suffering directly influences our moral decisions.

Adam Smith, often known for his economic theories, also delved deeply into the role of empathy in ethics. In his theory, the "impartial spectator" process involves stepping into another's shoes and judging our own and others' actions from an empathetic standpoint. Smith posited that this capacity for empathy underpins all human interactions and is fundamental to the social fabric.

Nineteenth and Twentieth Century Developments

In the nineteenth century, empathy started to be studied not just philosophically but also psychologically. The German philosopher Theodor Lipps introduced the concept of "Einfühlung" (literally, "feeling into"), which later translated into the English word "empathy." Lipps' theory suggested that aesthetic appreciation involved projecting one's own emotional state onto objects and works of art, thereby extending the scope of empathy beyond interpersonal relationships.

The 20th century saw further expansion in the study of empathy, influenced by psychological and neuroscientific discoveries. The development of psychological theories like those of Carl Rogers emphasized empathy as a core component of effective psychotherapy, promoting an understanding that goes beyond cognitive awareness to a deep, affective sharing of experiences.

Contemporary Perspectives and Challenges

Today, the discussion of empathy continues to evolve, particularly as global connectivity and social media change the ways in which we interact with and understand others. Current ethical discussions around empathy also face challenges related to empathy fatigue, the ethics of care, and the implications of empathetic biases.

Empathy's journey through history reveals its integral role in shaping ethical thought and human relationships. By understanding its historical development, we can appreciate the complexity of empathy and its enduring importance in promoting ethical behavior and mutual understanding across different cultures and societies. This historical perspective not only enriches our understanding of empathy but also highlights its potential to foster a more compassionate and ethical world.

ppp

"Empathy is the silent force that heals wounds unseen, binds hearts broken, and reminds us of our shared humanity amidst the cacophony of life's trials."

ﭏﭏﭏ

FIVE

The Role of Empathy in Family Dynamics

Empathy plays a pivotal role in family dynamics, serving as the emotional connective tissue that binds family members together. Within the family context, empathy influences how relationships develop, how conflicts are resolved, and how members support one another through life's challenges.

Building Strong Bonds in Early Childhood

The foundation of empathetic family dynamics is often laid in early childhood. Parents who exhibit empathy towards their children teach them, through modeling, how to recognize and respond to emotional cues. This early parental empathy fosters secure attachment relationships, which are crucial for the child's emotional and social development.

For instance, when a parent sensitively and appropriately responds to a baby's needs, the child learns that the world is a safe place where they can express their feelings and needs without fear of rejection or punishment. This early experience shapes the child's ability to empathize with others as they grow, influencing their social interactions and emotional well-being.

Empathy in Parenting Practices

As children grow, the role of empathy in parenting evolves but remains central. Empathetic parenting involves understanding the child's perspective and emotional state, even as these become more complex. This practice helps parents guide their children through the challenges of growing up, from navigating school pressures to managing friendships and personal identity.

Empathetic parents are more likely to use understanding and dialogue rather than punishment when addressing behavioral issues, which promotes problem-solving and emotional regulation skills in children. For example, a parent might ask why a child acted out, rather than immediately resorting to disciplinary measures, fostering a more open and communicative relationship.

Sibling Relationships and Empathy

Empathy also affects the dynamics between siblings. Empathetic siblings can provide significant emotional support, teach social skills, and help manage conflicts within the family. When siblings engage empathetically with each other, they develop a deep sense of camaraderie and trust that can last a lifetime.

Conversely, a lack of empathy among siblings can lead to rivalry and conflict. Therefore, parents often play a crucial role in fostering empathy between siblings by encouraging them to understand and care for each other's feelings and perspectives.

Empathy During Family Conflicts

Conflict is inevitable in any family, but empathy can be a critical tool for resolution. When family members strive to understand each other's viewpoints and emotions during disagreements, they can find solutions that respect everyone's needs rather than win-lose outcomes.

Empathy in conflict involves active listening, validation of feelings, and a genuine effort to understand the other's perspective. For instance, during a dispute about household responsibilities, family members can use empathy to understand each other's workload and stress levels, leading to a fairer distribution of tasks that acknowledges everyone's capacity and contributions.

Empathy in Times of Family Crisis

Families often face crises—such as illness, financial hardship, or loss—that test their strength and cohesiveness. Empathy becomes especially vital during these times. An empathetic family can provide a supportive environment where members feel understood and cared for, which is essential for navigating through tough periods.

When a family member is ill, for instance, empathy from other family members can alleviate feelings of isolation and despair, offering the emotional sustenance needed for recovery. This support might involve understanding the need for quiet, providing physical care, or offering words of encouragement.

Empathy Across Generations

Another important aspect of family empathy involves intergenerational relationships. Empathy allows family members to bridge the age gap between children, parents, and grandparents.

By empathizing with the unique challenges and experiences of different generations, family members can foster mutual respect and learning.

For example, young adults might use empathy to understand their aging parents' struggles with health and independence, while parents can empathize with their young adult children's challenges in navigating modern life pressures. This mutual understanding can enhance the support each generation provides to the other, enriching the family's emotional landscape.

Empathy within the family is not just beneficial but essential. It enables family members to build and maintain strong, supportive relationships that can adapt to the changes and challenges of life. By prioritizing empathy in family interactions, families can create a nurturing environment that promotes the well-being and development of all its members, contributing to a legacy of understanding and closeness that can influence generations.

ᐅᐅᐅ

"In the tapestry of human experience, empathy is
the golden thread that weaves hearts together,
creating a fabric of understanding, acceptance, and
love."

♥♥♥

SIX

EMPATHY AT WORK: BUILDING BETTER RELATIONSHIPS

In the modern workplace, empathy is increasingly recognized as a key driver of success, contributing to stronger relationships, enhanced collaboration, and improved workplace culture. Empathy in the workplace goes beyond just understanding colleagues' feelings; it involves actively engaging with their perspectives and experiences to foster a more supportive and effective work environment.

Enhancing Leadership with Empathy

Leaders who demonstrate empathy are better equipped to motivate their teams, foster loyalty, and improve overall performance. Empathetic leadership involves recognizing the emotions of team members, understanding their challenges both in and outside of work, and responding appropriately to their needs.

An empathetic leader will take the time to listen to their employees, understand the stresses and pressures they face, and provide support or flexibility where needed. For example, acknowledging an employee's workload and offering practical support or adjusting deadlines demonstrates understanding and consideration for their situation, which can increase job satisfaction and loyalty.

Empathy in Team Dynamics

Empathy plays a crucial role in team dynamics, facilitating smoother collaboration and conflict resolution. In teams, empathy helps members to understand each other's viewpoints and work styles, which can enhance coordination and reduce misunderstandings.

For instance, in a project team, if a member is struggling with a particular task, empathetic colleagues will recognize the need for support rather than judgment. This could lead to offering help or resources, or simply providing moral support, which can help overcome the hurdle and strengthen the team's cohesion.

Empathy and Customer Relations

Empathy is also vital in managing customer relationships. An empathetic approach can lead to better understanding of customers' needs and expectations, enabling more effective communication and service. This is particularly important in fields such as sales, customer service, and healthcare, where understanding the client or patient's perspective is crucial.

When dealing with a dissatisfied customer, an empathetic employee might acknowledge the customer's frustration, validate their feelings, and then work towards a solution. This not only helps in resolving the immediate issue but also builds trust and loyalty, which are essential for long-term customer relationships.

Empathy and Organizational Culture

The broader organizational culture greatly benefits from empathy. A culture that values and promotes empathy is likely to be more inclusive and supportive, encouraging employees from diverse backgrounds to share their ideas and perspectives. This can lead to more innovative solutions and a more adaptable organization.

Creating an empathetic culture starts at the top. When leaders model empathetic behavior, it sets a precedent for the entire organization. This might include policies that support work-life balance, training programs that enhance emotional intelligence, or regular check-ins with employees to understand their needs and concerns.

Empathy, Diversity, and Inclusion

Empathy is a key component in driving diversity and inclusion in the workplace. It allows employees to appreciate and embrace differences, which enhances team performance and innovation. By understanding and valuing the diverse experiences of all employees, organizations can create a more equitable and dynamic work environment.

For example, empathetic engagement with employees from different cultural backgrounds can help in understanding unique perspectives and needs, which can inform more effective management strategies and policy-making. This not only improves employee satisfaction but also attracts talent from diverse pools, enriching the organization's capabilities.

Empathy and Personal Development

Finally, empathy contributes to personal development within the workplace. Employees who practice empathy develop better communication skills, emotional intelligence, and problem-solving abilities. These skills are valuable not only in their current roles but also in their broader career progression.

Practicing empathy might involve seeking feedback on one's work, showing genuine interest in colleagues' projects, or sharing credit for success. These behaviors not only improve individual performance but also enhance professional relationships, making the workplace more collaborative and enjoyable.

Embedding empathy into the fabric of workplace operations and culture has profound benefits. It enhances leadership effectiveness, improves team dynamics, fosters a positive organizational culture, and drives diversity and inclusion. By prioritizing empathy, organizations can not only improve their operational efficiency but also create a more supportive, innovative, and resilient workplace.

ᐯᐯᐯ

"To empathize is to walk in another's shoes, to feel
the earth beneath their feet, and to see the world
through their eyes, knowing that in their journey,
lies the essence of our own."

❥❥❥

SEVEN

Cultural Differences in Expressing Empathy

Empathy, while a universal human trait, is expressed and valued differently across various cultures. These variations can affect interpersonal interactions, workplace dynamics, and even international relations. Understanding these cultural differences in empathy is crucial for fostering effective communication and cooperation in our increasingly globalized world.

Defining Cultural Empathy

Cultural empathy refers to the ability to recognize, understand, and appropriately respond to people from different cultural backgrounds based on an understanding of their cultural norms, beliefs, and practices. This form of empathy extends beyond emotional or cognitive empathy by incorporating a cultural dimension that considers the context of the other person's behaviors and feelings.

Individualism vs. Collectivism

One of the most significant factors influencing how empathy is expressed is the distinction between individualistic and collectivistic cultures. Individualistic cultures, such as those in the United States and Western Europe, tend to emphasize personal autonomy and self-expression. In these cultures, empathy might be expressed through direct support or validation of an individual's feelings and experiences.

In contrast, collectivistic cultures, which are prevalent in many Asian and African countries, emphasize group harmony and social cohesion. In these contexts, empathy is often expressed in more subdued and indirect ways, prioritizing the group's well-being over individual expression. For example, rather than directly addressing someone's emotional distress, people in collectivistic cultures might choose to act in ways that restore harmony without explicitly acknowledging the emotional issue.

High-Context vs. Low-Context Communication

The concept of high-context and low-context communication also plays a crucial role in how empathy is expressed. High-context cultures (e.g., Japan, China) rely heavily on non-verbal cues, implicit messages, and the overall context to communicate. In these cultures, empathy is often communicated through actions rather than words, and understanding these subtle signals requires a deep understanding of the cultural context.

Low-context cultures (e.g., Germany, Sweden), on the other hand, value explicit communication and directness. Empathy in these cultures is often expressed through clear verbal support and direct acknowledgment of another person's feelings.

Power Distance

Power distance, the degree to which less powerful members of a society accept and expect that power is distributed unequally, influences empathic interactions as well. In cultures with high power distance, such as Malaysia or Mexico, empathy might be expressed differently across hierarchical lines, with subordinates showing greater deference to the emotional cues of their superiors.

In low power distance cultures, like Denmark and New Zealand, there is a more egalitarian view of power distribution, and empathy is more likely to be expressed openly and reciprocally across different levels of a hierarchy.

Role of Religion and Tradition

Religious beliefs and traditional values also shape how empathy is perceived and practiced. For example, in many Middle Eastern cultures, Islamic teachings influence empathetic behaviors, emphasizing compassion and support within the community. Similarly, Buddhist cultures may view empathy as a path to enlightenment, stressing the importance of compassion and suffering with others.

Age and Gender Roles

Cultural norms around age and gender also affect how empathy is expressed. In some cultures, older individuals may be expected to be more stoic and less openly empathetic, whereas, in others, age might confer the freedom to express empathy more openly. Gender roles can also influence empathetic expression; in many societies, women are expected to be more empathetic and nurturing than men, impacting how empathy is both expressed and received.

Globalization and Cultural Empathy

With globalization, the need for cultural empathy has become more acute as people from diverse cultures increasingly come into contact through travel, migration, and communication technologies. Multinational organizations, in particular, must navigate these varied empathetic expressions to build cohesive and effective teams composed of members from different cultural backgrounds.

Understanding the cultural nuances of empathy is essential for anyone working across cultural boundaries. By recognizing and respecting these differences, individuals and organizations can foster deeper mutual understanding and cooperation, enhancing both personal and professional relationships in a globally connected world.

ᛈᛈᛈ

"Empathy is not a solitary act but a symphony of emotions, where each note played resonates with the harmonies of compassion, kindness, and understanding."

❥❥❥

EIGHT

THE CHALLENGES OF EMPATHY: OVERCOMING EMPATHIC DISTRESS"

While empathy is a valuable trait that can enhance interpersonal relationships and promote understanding, it also comes with its own set of challenges. One of the most significant of these is empathic distress, a condition where an individual feels overwhelmed by the emotions of others. This can lead to burnout, emotional exhaustion, and a decrease in the ability to empathize effectively. Understanding and overcoming these challenges is crucial for maintaining healthy emotional boundaries and continuing to offer empathy in a sustainable way.

Understanding Empathic Distress

Empathic distress occurs when an individual's emotional response to the suffering of others becomes so intense that it starts to impede their ability to function. This can happen to healthcare providers, caregivers, social workers, and anyone who regularly deals with the emotional burdens of others. The distress manifests as feelings of sadness, anxiety, and emotional exhaustion, leading to a state where the person's own well-being is compromised.

Differentiating Between Empathy and Over-Identification

A key factor in managing empathic distress is differentiating between healthy empathy and over-identification. Empathy involves understanding and sharing the feelings of another without losing sight of the distinction between self and other. Over-identification, however, occurs when individuals become so absorbed in another's experience that they begin to lose their own emotional equilibrium. This can lead to a blurring of boundaries and make individuals feel as though they are experiencing the traumas or stress of others firsthand.

Strategies for Managing Empathic Distress

Setting Emotional Boundaries

One effective way to combat empathic distress is through the establishment of clear emotional boundaries. This means understanding where one's emotions end and another's begin. Practicing mindfulness and self-awareness can help individuals recognize when they are taking on too much of another's emotional load and allow them to step back and regain their emotional center.

Self-Care and Resilience Building

Self-care is an essential strategy for anyone regularly exposed to the emotional stresses of others. This can include physical activities like exercise, hobbies that distract and soothe, or simply ensuring adequate rest and nutrition. Psychological self-care, such as meditation or therapy, can also play a crucial role in maintaining emotional health and resilience.

Professional Support

For professionals in high-empathy fields like healthcare or social work, institutional support can be crucial. This might include supervision where feelings and experiences are discussed, workshops on managing emotional boundaries, or peer support groups. These resources can provide valuable strategies for managing empathic distress and prevent burnout.

Education and Training

Educating oneself about the signs of empathic distress and the techniques for managing it can also be highly beneficial. Training in emotional intelligence can enhance a person's ability to regulate their emotions and improve their responses to emotionally charged situations. This not only helps in managing empathic distress but also in enhancing overall empathetic engagement.

The Role of Compassionate Empathy

Switching from empathic distress to compassionate empathy is another effective strategy. While empathic distress involves taking on others' emotional pain, compassionate empathy focuses on maintaining a helpful distance and thinking about how one can best assist the other person. This shift allows individuals to feel concern and take helpful action without becoming overwhelmed by negative emotions.

Building a Sustainable Practice of Empathy

Creating a sustainable practice of empathy involves balancing one's emotional inputs and outputs. Regularly assessing one's emotional state and adjusting interactions with others to maintain this balance can help manage the challenges of empathy effectively. It's also helpful to recognize when to seek help, whether from colleagues, friends, or mental health professionals, to discuss and manage feelings of empathic distress.

Empathy is an invaluable human capacity that enhances personal relationships and professional interactions. However, managing the challenges associated with it, particularly empathic distress, is crucial for those who work in empathy-heavy professions or find themselves frequently overwhelmed by the emotions of others. By adopting strategies such as setting emotional boundaries, engaging in self-care, seeking professional support, and fostering compassionate empathy, individuals can continue to offer empathy in a way that is both effective and sustainable.

▷▷▷

"In the garden of empathy, seeds of kindness
blossom into flowers of connection, nurturing
relationships that bloom with authenticity,
vulnerability, and love."

🖤🖤🖤

NINE

Technology and Empathy: Virtual Connections, Real Feelings

In the digital age, technology plays a pivotal role in shaping how we connect and empathize with others. From social media platforms to virtual reality experiences, technological innovations have both expanded and complicated the ways in which we understand and share the feelings of others. Exploring how these digital tools influence empathy can help us harness them more effectively to foster genuine human connections.

Social Media and Empathy

Social media platforms like Facebook, Twitter, and Instagram have transformed the landscape of human interaction. These platforms allow us to share our lives and empathize with others across great distances. However, the nature of these connections often raises questions about the depth and authenticity of the empathy expressed online.

On one hand, social media can promote empathy by providing insights into the lives and struggles of diverse groups of people. Campaigns around social issues and personal stories shared on these platforms can elicit widespread empathetic responses from a global audience. For instance, hashtag movements such as #MeToo have brought shared experiences of harassment and assault into the public eye, fostering a collective sense of empathy and solidarity.

On the other hand, the brief and often superficial interactions on social media may lead to what some call "slacktivism" — a low-effort, minimal impact engagement that feels empathetic but does not translate into real-world action. Additionally, the algorithms that curate content on these platforms can create echo chambers that reinforce our own viewpoints, potentially reducing our exposure to diverse perspectives and thus limiting our empathetic growth.

Virtual Reality and Empathy

Virtual reality (VR) offers an even more immersive technological experience that has significant implications for empathy. VR can literally place individuals in someone else's shoes, offering first-person experiences of other people's lives and challenges. For example, VR experiences that simulate the life of a refugee or a person living with a disability can produce profound empathetic responses and increase understanding and compassion among users.

The power of VR lies in its ability to evoke a strong emotional connection by making distant or abstract issues feel immediate and real. This has been used effectively in educational settings, therapy, and awareness campaigns, suggesting that VR could be a powerful tool for cultivating empathy on a wide scale.

Messaging and Communication Technologies

The rise of instant messaging apps and communication technologies has also transformed how we express empathy. Text messages, emails, and video calls enable us to maintain personal connections and offer support instantaneously, even from afar. However, these modes of communication come with their own challenges for empathetic interaction.

The lack of non-verbal cues in text-based communication can make it difficult to convey or interpret empathy effectively. Misunderstandings are common, and the tone can be easily misread. Emojis and GIFs have evolved as tools to help express emotions and intentions more clearly, but they are imperfect substitutes for face-to-face interaction.

Video calls offer a richer medium through which to communicate, providing visual and auditory cues that can enhance empathetic understanding. They have become especially important in maintaining personal and professional relationships in situations where in-person interactions are not possible, such as during the COVID-19 pandemic.

The Ethical Dimensions of Technology and Empathy

As technology reshapes our empathetic interactions, it also raises significant ethical questions. The data collected by social media platforms and other digital tools can be used to manipulate users' emotions and opinions, raising concerns about privacy and consent. Moreover, the design of these technologies often prioritizes engagement over genuine connection, potentially leading to negative effects on mental health.

Addressing these ethical challenges requires a critical examination of how these technologies are designed and used. It calls for the development of digital tools that enhance real empathetic connections without compromising individual autonomy or well-being.

Technology has a profound impact on empathy, offering new ways to connect and understand each other but also presenting significant challenges. By critically engaging with these tools and considering their effects on our emotional lives, we can better navigate the digital landscape to foster deeper and more meaningful empathetic connections. Whether through social media, virtual reality, or instant messaging, the goal remains the same: to enhance our capacity to empathize with others in a way that enriches our relationships and our society.

ϸϸϸ

"The essence of empathy lies not in fixing others'
problems but in holding their hands, walking
alongside them, and whispering, 'You are not alone;
I am here.'"

❧❧❧

TEN

TEACHING EMPATHY: STRATEGIES FOR EDUCATORS AND PARENTS

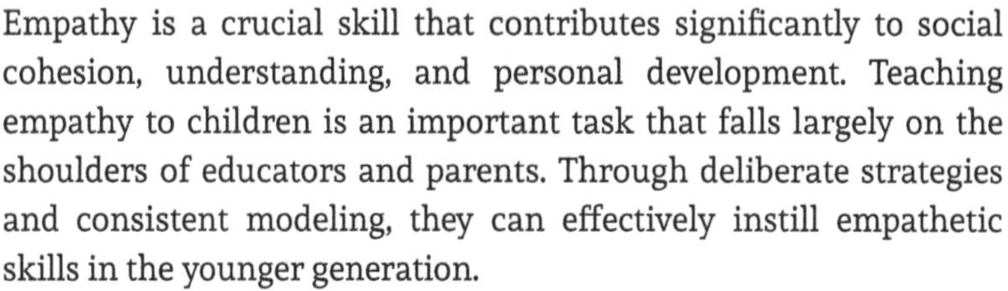

Empathy is a crucial skill that contributes significantly to social cohesion, understanding, and personal development. Teaching empathy to children is an important task that falls largely on the shoulders of educators and parents. Through deliberate strategies and consistent modeling, they can effectively instill empathetic skills in the younger generation.

Understanding Developmental Stages

Empathy develops in stages as children grow. Young children start by recognizing their own emotions and gradually begin to understand that others have separate feelings and perspectives. Educators and parents can tailor their approach to teaching empathy by considering these developmental stages, ensuring that the methods and lessons are age-appropriate and engaging.

Role-Modeling Empathetic Behavior

Children learn a great deal from observing the behavior of adults. When educators and parents consistently display empathy in their interactions with others, children absorb these behaviors and emulate them. This includes showing compassion in everyday situations, discussing feelings openly, and demonstrating how to listen actively and respond thoughtfully to others.

Creating an Inclusive Classroom Environment

Teachers can foster empathy by creating a classroom culture where all students feel valued and understood. This involves promoting inclusiveness, respecting diverse backgrounds, and addressing any forms of bullying or exclusion. Activities that encourage students to explore different perspectives, such as reading books from varied cultures or discussing historical events from multiple viewpoints, can also enhance empathetic understanding.

Empathy-Based Conflict Resolution

Incorporating empathy into conflict resolution teaches children how to handle disputes fairly and compassionately. Educators can guide students through the process of identifying emotions, articulating their feelings, and considering the feelings of others involved in a conflict. This not only resolves the immediate issue but also equips students with valuable social skills for the future.

Collaborative Projects

Group projects that require collaboration can be excellent

opportunities for practicing empathy. These activities encourage students to understand their peers' strengths and weaknesses, work together towards common goals, and support each other's learning. Teachers can facilitate this by setting clear roles, encouraging open communication, and providing feedback on how effectively the group is working together.

Everyday Empathy

Parents can teach empathy by incorporating it into daily interactions. This includes discussing feelings at the dinner table, showing how to respond to family members' or friends' emotional needs, and even reflecting on characters' emotions while reading stories or watching movies together.

Emotional Vocabulary

Expanding a child's emotional vocabulary is another powerful tool. By teaching children the words to express their feelings, parents help them to identify and communicate their emotions more effectively. This also aids children in recognizing and naming the emotions of others, a fundamental aspect of empathy.

Experiential Learning

Parents can create opportunities for children to experience empathy firsthand. This might involve community service projects, such as volunteering at a local food bank or participating in community clean-up days. Experiences like these can help children understand the circumstances and challenges that others face, deepening their empathetic feelings.

Supporting Empathy Through Technology

In the digital age, parents and educators can also utilize technology to teach empathy. Educational apps and games that simulate social interactions can be effective tools, especially for older children and teenagers. These digital platforms can provide safe spaces for young people to explore emotional dynamics and the consequences of different actions in a controlled, guided environment.

Encouraging Reflective Practices

Both educators and parents can encourage children to engage in reflective practices. This might involve having children think about how their actions affect others or discussing the outcomes of specific empathetic or non-empathetic behaviors. Reflection helps solidify learning and can make empathetic behavior more of a natural response in children's future interactions.

Teaching empathy is a vital endeavor that requires thoughtful strategies and consistent application by both educators and parents. By modeling empathetic behavior, creating supportive environments, and using appropriate tools and activities, they can significantly influence the development of empathy in children. This not only benefits the children themselves but also contributes to a more compassionate and understanding society.

ᗐᗐᗐ

"Empathy is the art of seeing beyond the surface,
peering into the depths of another's soul, and
finding reflections of our own hopes, fears, and
dreams."

ԲԲԲ

ELEVEN

THE DARK SIDE OF EMPATHY: WHEN IT HURTS TO CARE

Empathy, widely regarded as a positive trait that enhances interpersonal relationships and fosters understanding, sometimes reveals a more complex and darker aspect. While it allows individuals to connect deeply with others, excessive empathy can lead to emotional burnout, skewed decision-making, and interpersonal conflicts. Understanding the darker sides of empathy is crucial for managing its impact effectively in our personal and professional lives.

The Burden of Emotional Contagion

Empathy involves resonating with another person's emotional state, a process sometimes described as emotional contagion. This can be psychologically taxing, particularly for individuals who frequently encounter emotional distress or trauma in others, such as healthcare professionals, therapists, and social workers. The continuous exposure to suffering can lead to empathic distress or secondary traumatic stress, where the observer begins to experience trauma symptoms themselves.

This emotional contagion is not limited to professional settings. It can also occur in personal relationships, where one person may become so absorbed in the emotional upheavals of another that their own well-being starts to suffer. This can lead to a state of chronic stress, affecting mental health and leading to conditions like anxiety and depression.

The Pitfalls of Altruism

Empathy can drive altruistic behavior, motivating individuals to help others even at a cost to themselves. However, this altruism can become problematic when it leads to self-neglect or when the desire to help is manipulated by others. In some cases, highly empathetic individuals may become targets for exploitation, as their strong desire to help can make them overlook their own needs and boundaries.

Moreover, excessive altruism can sometimes lead to ineffective or even harmful outcomes. For example, well-meaning efforts to help can sometimes disempower those they are meant to assist, leading to dependency rather than empowerment. Understanding the balance between helping and enabling is crucial in ensuring that empathetic actions are truly beneficial.

Empathy and Moral Judgments

Empathy can also complicate moral judgments. While it can enhance ethical decision-making by considering the feelings and needs of others, it can also bias individuals towards those they empathize with more strongly. This partiality can lead to ethical dilemmas where the needs of the few outweigh the needs of the many, or where certain groups receive more attention and resources simply because they elicit more empathy.

For instance, empathy might lead someone to lie or bend rules to help a friend in distress, compromising their own ethical standards. In larger-scale scenarios, like policymaking or charitable donations, empathy-driven decisions might prioritize well-publicized or emotionally striking issues over more pressing but less emotionally engaging needs.

Managing Empathy Effectively

Given the potential downsides of empathy, learning to manage it effectively is essential. This involves setting emotional boundaries to prevent burnout, practicing self-care to maintain one's own well-being, and developing critical thinking skills to balance empathetic impulses with rational decision-making.

One effective strategy is cultivating a type of empathy known as "compassionate empathy" or "empathic concern," which combines understanding another's pain with an appropriate level of detachment. This form of empathy motivates helpful action but with emotional boundaries that prevent over-identification with the sufferer.

Cultivating Healthy Emotional Boundaries

Creating healthy emotional boundaries is key to managing the darker sides of empathy. This means recognizing when to engage empathetically and when to step back, maintaining a balance between caring for others and preserving one's own emotional health. Techniques like mindfulness and reflective practices can help individuals recognize and modulate their emotional responses.

While empathy is undeniably a valuable trait, its darker aspects must be acknowledged and managed. By understanding the complexities of empathy, individuals can enjoy the benefits of connecting with others without succumbing to the emotional pitfalls it can entail. This balanced approach allows for sustaining healthy relationships, making ethical decisions, and maintaining personal well-being in a world where empathy is both a gift and a challenge.

ᲧᲧᲧ

"In moments of darkness, empathy is the guiding
light that illuminates the path forward, showing us
that even in our struggles, we are never truly
alone."

❥❥❥

TWELVE
EMPATHY AND LEADERSHIP: GUIDING WITH COMPASSION"

In the realm of leadership, empathy is increasingly recognized as a critical component for effective guidance and management. An empathetic leader is someone who understands the emotions of their team, can communicate effectively, and fosters a supportive work environment that encourages both personal and professional growth. This chapter delves into how empathy influences leadership and the strategies leaders can employ to harness its potential fully.

Understanding the Impact of Empathetic Leadership

Empathetic leadership goes beyond simply recognizing employees' feelings; it involves actively engaging with these emotions to inspire and motivate. Leaders who exhibit empathy are typically seen as more approachable and trustworthy, which can enhance team loyalty and overall morale. Moreover, such leaders are often better at conflict resolution and can navigate workplace challenges more smoothly, ensuring that the team's objectives are met with less friction and increased cooperation.

Benefits of Empathetic Leadership

Empathetic leadership brings several tangible benefits to the workplace:

Improved Team Collaboration: When team members feel understood and valued, they are more likely to contribute openly and collaborate effectively. Empathetic leaders foster an environment of mutual respect, where diverse opinions and ideas are welcomed and integrated into the decision-making process.

Enhanced Employee Retention: Workplaces led by empathetic leaders often experience lower turnover rates. Employees are more likely to feel satisfied and valued in their roles, reducing the desire to seek alternative employment.

Boosted Employee Engagement: Empathy helps leaders connect with their employees on a personal level, which can increase engagement and dedication to the organization's goals. Engaged employees are more productive and proactive in their contributions.

Stronger Change Management: Implementing change can be challenging, but empathetic leaders can ease this process by understanding and addressing the concerns and anxieties that change might provoke among team members.

Developing Empathetic Leadership Skills

Becoming an empathetic leader involves a combination of self-awareness, active listening, and genuine concern for the well-being of others. Here are some strategies for developing these skills:

Self-awareness

Leaders must first understand their own emotions and how they affect their behavior. Self-awareness allows leaders to manage their responses and approach situations calmly and objectively. Techniques such as mindfulness meditation and reflective journaling can help leaders gain deeper insights into their emotional triggers and responses.

Active Listening

Active listening is a key skill for empathetic leaders. It involves fully concentrating on the speaker, understanding their message, responding thoughtfully, and remembering the information later. This not only helps in gathering valuable insights but also shows respect and appreciation for the team members' input.

Emotional Intelligence Training

Many organizations now offer training in emotional intelligence, which includes developing empathy. These programs often cover understanding and managing one's emotions, recognizing the emotions of others, and using this awareness to guide interactions and decisions.

Regular Feedback

Creating a feedback-rich environment can enhance empathetic leadership. This involves not just providing feedback to employees but also soliciting feedback about one's leadership style. Such openness to feedback can improve a leader's approach and demonstrate their commitment to personal and professional growth.

Challenges and Considerations

While the benefits of empathetic leadership are significant, there are challenges too. Too much empathy can sometimes hinder decision-making, particularly when tough choices need to be made that might negatively affect individuals. Leaders must learn to balance empathy with decisiveness, ensuring that their compassion does not cloud their judgment.

Furthermore, empathy needs to be genuine. Feigned empathy can be easily detected and may lead to distrust and cynicism among team members. Thus, leaders must cultivate a true sense of empathy, which is consistent and evident in their actions and decisions.

Empathy is a powerful tool in a leader's arsenal, capable of transforming workplace dynamics, enhancing team performance, and improving organizational outcomes. By fostering an empathetic leadership style, leaders can build more cohesive and resilient teams equipped to face the complexities of the modern business environment. True empathetic leadership not only improves the well-being of employees but also sets the stage for sustained success and growth.

"Empathy is the compass that guides us through the labyrinth of human emotions, leading us toward understanding, connection, and ultimately, healing."

ᗽᗽᗽ

THIRTEEN

EMPATHY IN LITERATURE AND ART: REFLECTING HUMAN EXPERIENCE

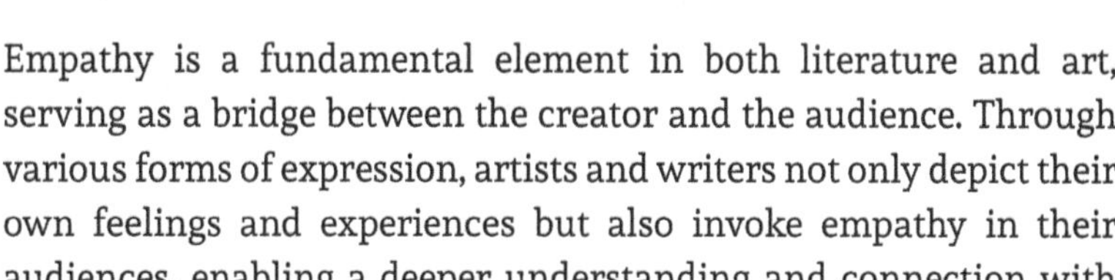

Empathy is a fundamental element in both literature and art, serving as a bridge between the creator and the audience. Through various forms of expression, artists and writers not only depict their own feelings and experiences but also invoke empathy in their audiences, enabling a deeper understanding and connection with the work. This exploration of human emotions and situations helps to broaden the audience's perspective, deepening their understanding of others.

Empathy in Literature

In literature, empathy allows readers to connect with characters' inner lives, understanding their motivations, emotions, and struggles. This empathetic connection is crucial for the immersive experience that literature offers. Authors employ various narrative techniques to evoke empathy, including detailed character development, first-person narratives, and emotive language.

Character Development

Through complex character development, authors give readers insight into the thoughts and feelings of the characters. By presenting characters with depth and nuances, authors make them relatable and real, which encourages readers to empathize with their journeys. For instance, in Harper Lee's *To Kill a Mockingbird*, the moral struggles and development of characters like Atticus Finch allow readers to explore their own beliefs about justice and morality.

First-Person Narratives

First-person narratives can be particularly effective in evoking empathy. By allowing readers to see the world through the characters' eyes, authors help readers to live vicariously through the experiences narrated. Books like Sylvia Plath's *The Bell Jar* provide a deeply personal view of the protagonist's mind, giving readers a visceral sense of her psychological struggles.

Emotive Language

The use of emotive language enhances the ability of literature to evoke empathy. Descriptive passages that capture the emotions of scenes or the inner turmoil of characters help to engage the reader's feelings, making the narrative more compelling and empathetic.

Empathy in Visual Arts

In the realm of visual arts, empathy plays a crucial role in connecting the viewer with the subject matter or the emotions the artist intends to convey. Artists use colors, forms, and symbols to communicate feelings and experiences, often leaving a lasting impact on the viewer.

Portraiture

Portraiture is a direct way in which artists explore empathy. By capturing the expressions and emotions of the subjects, portraits can convey a profound sense of the person's inner life. Works like those of Frida Kahlo, for example, not only depict her physical appearance but also her emotional pain and resilience, inviting viewers to empathize with her experiences.

Symbolism and Color

Artists also use symbolism and color to evoke specific emotions or to symbolize certain feelings, which can foster empathy. The use of dark, intense colors might communicate feelings of despair or melancholy, while bright, warm colors might convey happiness or optimism. The choice of colors and symbols can guide the emotional responses of the audience, enhancing their empathetic engagement with the artwork.

Empathy in Performance Arts

In performance arts such as theater and film, empathy is crucial for the audience's emotional engagement. Actors employ body language, tone of voice, and facial expressions to convey their characters' emotions, which can elicit empathetic responses from the audience.

Method Acting

Method acting is a technique used by actors to achieve deep levels of empathy for their characters. By living and experiencing the life of the character they are portraying, actors aim to genuinely feel their characters' emotions, which in turn enhances the authenticity of their performances. This authenticity can resonate deeply with audiences, allowing them to empathize with the characters on a profound level.

Empathy in literature and art not only enhances the audience's engagement with works but also serves a larger purpose of fostering understanding and connection among people. Through empathetic engagement with characters, narratives, and artistic expressions, individuals can explore complex human emotions and experiences. This not only enriches the audience's personal life but also enhances societal empathy, contributing to a more compassionate world. By reflecting human experiences in a relatable way, literature and art play a pivotal role in the human capacity to understand and connect with others.

ᕤᕤᕤ

"In a world filled with noise, empathy is the quiet
voice that speaks volumes, echoing across hearts
and minds with the timeless message of
compassion."

♡♡♡

FOURTEEN

EMPATHIC COMMUNICATION: BEYOND WORDS

Empathic communication transcends mere words, involving a deep level of understanding and connection that can significantly enhance interpersonal relationships. It's a comprehensive approach to interaction that involves listening, responding, and connecting in a way that goes beyond the spoken language. This type of communication is crucial in building trust, resolving conflicts, and fostering deeper bonds between individuals.

Understanding Non-Verbal Elements of Empathy

Non-verbal communication plays a pivotal role in conveying empathy. This includes facial expressions, body language, eye contact, and even silence. Each of these elements can communicate a person's attention, understanding, and care without a single word being spoken.

Facial Expressions

Facial expressions are powerful conveyors of emotions. A concerned look, a warm smile, or a furrowed brow can communicate empathy more effectively than words alone. These expressions can make the speaker feel seen and understood, which is central to empathic communication.

Body Language

Body language also significantly impacts how empathic communication is perceived. Open body postures, such as uncrossed arms, nodding, and leaning forward, suggest openness and attentiveness. These cues can make the speaker feel that the listener is engaged and empathetic to their situation.

Eye Contact

Maintaining appropriate eye contact is another crucial aspect of non-verbal empathic communication. It shows the speaker that the listener is focused and present. However, cultural contexts must be considered, as the norms for eye contact can vary widely across different cultures.

The Role of Silence

Silence, when used appropriately, can be a powerful tool in empathic communication. It can provide space for the speaker to gather thoughts or express emotions, signaling that the listener is patient and open to understanding more deeply.

The Power of Active Listening

Active listening is at the heart of empathic communication. It involves fully concentrating on the speaker, understanding their message, responding thoughtfully, and remembering the conversation's content. Active listening demonstrates to the speaker that their words are valuable and that they are respected and understood.

Reflective Listening

Reflective listening, a key component of active listening, involves paraphrasing or summarizing what the speaker has said to ensure clarity and understanding. This technique not only confirms that the listener has understood but also helps the speaker see their thoughts and feelings validated.

Validating Emotions

Part of active listening involves acknowledging and validating the speaker's emotions. This doesn't mean agreeing with them but recognizing their feelings as real and valid. Such validation can relieve emotional tension and foster a deeper sense of connection.

Empathy in Written Communication

While much of empathic communication focuses on in-person interactions, written communication also holds the potential for empathy. This can be particularly important in digital communications, where traditional non-verbal cues are absent.

Choice of Words

In written communication, the choice of words becomes even more crucial. Using language that conveys understanding and concern can help bridge the emotional gap caused by the lack of non-verbal cues.

Tone and Style

The tone and style of written communication should convey warmth and empathy. This can involve using phrases that show care and concern, or simply ensuring the language is gentle and supportive.

Challenges in Empathic Communication

Despite its importance, empathic communication can be challenging. Misunderstandings can arise, especially when non-verbal cues are misinterpreted or cultural differences are overlooked.

Additionally, in high-stress situations, maintaining empathic communication requires patience and emotional intelligence.

Training and Development in Empathic Communication

Organizations and individuals can benefit from training in empathic communication. Workshops and courses can help develop the necessary skills to communicate empathically across various settings.

These training programs often cover emotional intelligence, active listening, conflict resolution, and non-verbal communication skills.

Empathic communication is a comprehensive approach that involves much more than just spoken words. It encompasses understanding, responding, and connecting through verbal and non-verbal means.

By mastering both aspects, individuals can enhance their personal and professional relationships, resolve conflicts more effectively, and build a foundation of trust and mutual respect. Whether through face-to-face interactions or digital communications, empathy remains a critical component of effective communication.

ϸϸϸ

"To empathize is to embrace vulnerability—to open our hearts to the rawness of human experience and to find strength in our shared imperfections."

❧❧❧

FIFTEEN

BUILDING EMPATHIC COMMUNITIES: FROM LOCAL TO GLOBAL"

Empathy serves as a foundational element in the construction of both cohesive local communities and inclusive global societies. By prioritizing empathic understanding and interactions, communities can foster environments that promote mutual respect, cooperation, and shared well-being. This endeavor involves initiatives at various levels, from local community projects to international cooperation, all aimed at enhancing empathy among diverse populations.

The Role of Empathy in Community Building

Empathy within a community context helps bridge the gaps between different social, economic, and cultural groups. It enables individuals to step beyond their own experiences and understand the lives and feelings of others within their community. This understanding is crucial for addressing communal challenges and conflicts, as it fosters a sense of shared humanity and mutual responsibility.

Initiatives at the Local Level

Local communities can foster empathy through various programs and initiatives that encourage social interaction and understanding across diverse groups.

Community Outreach Programs

These programs aim to connect individuals from different backgrounds through community service and engagement activities. By working together toward common goals, participants can learn about each other's lives and perspectives, which can break down prejudices and build empathetic connections.

Educational Programs

Schools and educational institutions play a critical role in cultivating empathy. Implementing curricula that include social and emotional learning (SEL) components can teach children from a young age the importance of empathy. Programs that emphasize history, literature, and cultural studies from multiple perspectives also enrich students' understanding of different life experiences.

Public Spaces and Events

Creating inclusive public spaces that encourage interaction among community members can also promote empathy. Libraries, parks, and community centers that host diverse cultural events provide opportunities for people to meet and share experiences, helping to foster a sense of community and mutual understanding.

Expanding to the National and Global Level

Building empathetic communities is not only a local endeavor but also a national and international one. The challenges of globalization and international conflicts make empathy more important than ever.

National Policies on Inclusion and Diversity

Governments can promote empathy through policies that ensure equal rights and opportunities for all citizens. Legislation that tackles discrimination and supports marginalized groups helps create a more empathetic society by acknowledging and addressing systemic inequalities.

International Aid and Cooperation

On a global scale, empathy is crucial for effective international aid and cooperation. Understanding the cultural and socio-economic contexts of aid recipients ensures that help provided is appropriate and effective. International partnerships based on mutual understanding and respect can lead to more sustainable outcomes and peace-building efforts.

Digital Platforms for Global Dialogue

In the age of digital communication, online platforms can serve as powerful tools for building global empathic connections. Social media, forums, and virtual exchange programs can connect individuals from around the world, allowing them to share stories and collaborate on global issues, fostering a worldwide community of empathy.

Overcoming Challenges in Empathic Community Building

While the benefits of building empathetic communities are significant, there are challenges to these efforts, primarily due to cultural differences, historical conflicts, and socioeconomic disparities.

Addressing Cultural Barriers

Effective communication across cultures requires understanding and respecting cultural differences. Training programs and workshops that focus on cultural competence can equip community leaders and members with the skills needed to engage empathetically with diverse populations.

Dealing with Conflicts

In areas with historical or ongoing conflicts, building empathy can be particularly challenging. Conflict resolution initiatives that use empathy-building as a core strategy can help rival groups understand each other's perspectives and work towards reconciliation.

Building empathetic communities, from the local to the global level, requires sustained effort and commitment across various sectors of society. By prioritizing empathy in educational systems, public policies, and everyday interactions, communities can create environments where understanding and cooperation thrive. These efforts not only enhance the quality of life within communities but also contribute to a more peaceful and connected global society.

ᡠᡠᡠ

"Empathy is the gift we give not only to others but also to ourselves—a reminder that in moments of pain and sorrow, we are capable of boundless love and resilience."

ᕱᕱᕱ

SIXTEEN

THE ETHICS OF CARE: PHILOSOPHICAL FOUNDATIONS"

The ethics of care is a philosophical framework that emphasizes the moral significance of our relationships and dependencies on others. It challenges the traditional ethical models that prioritize principles, rules, and individual rights, advocating instead for the centrality of interpersonal relationships and the virtues of care, responsiveness, and mutual support. This approach to ethics has profound implications for understanding how we interact with one another and how societies might structure their moral and legal obligations.

Historical and Conceptual Origins

The ethics of care emerged in the mid-20th century, with feminist thinkers critiquing the prevailing moral theories which they felt predominantly reflected male-centric perspectives. Carol Gilligan, a prominent psychologist, is often credited with pioneering this field with her critique of Lawrence Kohlberg's stages of moral development. Gilligan argued that Kohlberg's model was overly focused on concepts like justice and rights and did not adequately consider the moral reasoning that emphasizes interpersonal relationships and care.

Key Concepts in the Ethics of Care

Interdependence and Relationality

At the heart of the ethics of care is the recognition of the fundamental role of interdependence and relationality in human life. Unlike traditional moral theories that stress independence and detachment, care ethics sees humans as inherently relational beings whose identities are shaped by their relationships with others. This perspective encourages a morality that assesses situations and actions based not on abstract principles but on the nuances of human relationships.

Contextual Morality

The ethics of care advocates for a contextual approach to morality, arguing that ethical actions must always consider the specific contexts of situations. It rejects one-size-fits-all solutions, emphasizing instead the need to understand the particular details and relationships involved in each case. This approach allows for greater flexibility and responsiveness in moral decision-making.

Empathy and Responsiveness

Empathy is crucial in the ethics of care as it enables individuals to understand and respond to the needs of others effectively. Care ethics prioritizes empathetic engagement, which involves actively attending to another's experience and responding appropriately. This responsiveness is not just an emotional reaction but a principled and thoughtful approach to addressing others' needs.

The Role of Emotions

Unlike more traditional ethical models that often downplay the role of emotions in moral reasoning, the ethics of care recognizes emotions as a significant component of ethical understanding. Feelings such as compassion, empathy, and concern are seen as integral to discerning what care requires in any given situation, rather than as biases that cloud moral judgment.

Practical Implications of Care Ethics

The ethics of care has practical implications across various fields, including healthcare, education, and politics.

Healthcare

In healthcare, care ethics leads to a patient-centered approach that values the doctor-patient relationship and emphasizes care as a fundamental aspect of medical practice. This approach seeks to address the needs of the whole person rather than merely treating symptoms or diseases.

Education

In education, care ethics influences teaching methodologies by prioritizing relationships between teachers and students and among students themselves. It encourages an educational environment where students are cared for and learn to care for others, fostering a community of respect and mutual support.

Politics

Politically, care ethics advocates for policies and practices that reflect the interdependent nature of society. It supports social welfare programs that help meet the basic needs of all citizens, emphasizing the state's role in ensuring that vulnerable populations receive adequate care and support.

The ethics of care provides a robust framework for understanding and applying moral principles in a way that prioritizes human relationships, contextuality, and emotional engagement. By focusing on the interconnectedness of individuals and the importance of nurturing relationships, care ethics offers a compelling alternative to the more detached and principle-driven approaches that have traditionally dominated moral philosophy. It champions a more humane and responsive approach to ethics, one that is particularly suited to addressing the complex and varied needs of contemporary societies.

ᐅᐅᐅ

"In the tapestry of life, empathy is the golden
thread that binds us together, weaving a story of
compassion, connection, and belonging."

❦❦❦

SEVENTEEN
EMPATHY AND CONFLICT RESOLUTION: HEALING DIVIDES

Empathy plays a crucial role in conflict resolution by facilitating understanding and compassion among conflicting parties, ultimately helping to bridge divides and foster lasting peace. This approach to resolving disputes is essential in a range of contexts, from interpersonal relationships to international diplomacy.

Understanding Empathy in Conflict Resolution

Empathy in conflict resolution involves more than just feeling sorry for another person; it requires a deep understanding of the other party's emotions, perspectives, and motivations. This empathetic engagement allows for more effective communication and problem-solving because it promotes a mutual understanding that can pave the way for agreement and reconciliation.

The Mechanisms of Empathy in Conflict Resolution

Perspective Taking

Taking the perspective of another is a fundamental aspect of empathy in conflict resolution. This means trying to see the situation from the other person's point of view, which can help uncover underlying issues that are not apparent in confrontational exchanges. Understanding these deeper issues can lead to more comprehensive and enduring solutions.

Emotional Resonance

Emotional resonance allows individuals in conflict to feel the emotional states of others, which can decrease hostility and increase the willingness to cooperate. When parties in conflict recognize that their emotions are acknowledged and shared, they are more likely to engage in negotiations and less likely to escalate the conflict.

Communicating Understanding

Effective conflict resolution also involves communicating this understanding back to the other party. This reassurance that one's feelings and viewpoints are understood can build trust and openness, key ingredients for successful mediation and conflict resolution.

Implementing Empathy in Various Conflict Scenarios

In Personal Relationships

In personal relationships, conflicts often arise from misunderstandings or unmet emotional needs. Employing empathy by actively listening and validating the other person's feelings can help resolve these issues. For instance, in a family dispute, recognizing and articulating the emotions involved can lead to a better understanding of each family member's needs and expectations, thereby facilitating a more amicable resolution.

In the Workplace

Conflicts in the workplace can significantly disrupt productivity and morale. Managers and leaders who use empathic strategies can effectively mediate disputes by ensuring all parties feel heard and understood. This might involve group sessions where each person is encouraged to express their perspective and emotions related to the conflict, followed by collaborative problem-solving that includes input from all affected parties.

In Community and Societal Conflicts

Community and societal conflicts often involve complex issues such as race, religion, and politics. Empathy plays a critical role in these situations by humanizing the parties involved and reducing the us-versus-them mentality. Community leaders and facilitators can organize empathy-building activities like shared storytelling events, community dialogues, or joint community service projects to help break down barriers and build mutual understanding.

In International Relations

On the global stage, empathy is essential for resolving conflicts between nations. Diplomats and negotiators who employ empathy can better understand the motivations and fears of other nations, which can lead to more effective treaties and peace agreements.

Historical examples include peace talks that consider the cultural and historical contexts of the conflicting parties, helping to create solutions that respect the interests and dignity of all involved.

Challenges to Empathic Conflict Resolution

While empathy is a powerful tool for healing divides, its implementation is not without challenges. These include overcoming deep-seated prejudices, dealing with intense emotions, and the complexity of translating empathy into actionable solutions.

Overcoming Bias and Prejudice

Deep-seated biases and prejudices can hinder the ability to empathize with "the other." In such cases, facilitated discussions that focus on shared human experiences can help reduce these barriers and open the way for empathetic engagement.

Managing Emotional Intensity

Conflicts often involve intense emotions, which can be overwhelming. Training in emotional regulation can help individuals engage in empathetic listening and dialogue, even in emotionally charged situations.

Empathy is indispensable in the realm of conflict resolution. By fostering a deeper understanding and appreciation of differing perspectives and emotions, empathy has the power to transform conflicts at all levels—from personal disputes to global confrontations—into opportunities for growth and reconciliation.

The challenge lies in consistently applying empathetic principles in a world where conflict is often approached with hostility rather than understanding. However, with continued practice and commitment, empathy can lead to more peaceful and cooperative societies.

ƆƆƆ

"Empathy is the bridge that spans the chasm of
misunderstanding, connecting hearts and minds
with the timeless bonds of understanding and
compassion."

ᗽᗽᗽ

EIGHTEEN
EMPATHY IN HEALTHCARE: PATIENT-CENTERED APPROACHES

Empathy is a fundamental component of effective healthcare, enhancing patient care and improving clinical outcomes. A patient-centered approach that emphasizes empathy not only benefits patients but also healthcare providers, leading to a more satisfying and effective healthcare experience. This approach involves understanding patients' emotions, concerns, and perspectives, and integrating this understanding into all aspects of care.

The Importance of Empathy in Healthcare

Empathy in healthcare involves more than just good bedside manners; it's about making a genuine effort to understand patients' feelings and experiences and reflecting this understanding in how care is provided. This empathetic engagement can significantly impact patient satisfaction, adherence to treatment, and overall health outcomes.

Enhancing Patient Trust and Satisfaction

When patients feel that their healthcare providers genuinely care about them and are trying to understand their experiences and concerns, they are more likely to trust these providers. Trust is crucial for building a strong patient-provider relationship, which in turn can lead to increased patient satisfaction and loyalty.

Improving Treatment Adherence

Patients are more likely to follow treatment plans prescribed by empathetic providers. Understanding the patient's lifestyle, beliefs, and preferences can help providers tailor recommendations that patients are more willing to follow, thus improving adherence to treatments and interventions.

Reducing Malpractice Litigation

Studies have shown that empathy in healthcare can lead to a reduction in malpractice claims. When patients feel cared for and understood, they are less likely to feel neglected or wronged if an adverse outcome occurs.

Implementing Empathic Care in Various Healthcare Settings

Empathy should be woven into the fabric of healthcare practices, from primary care to specialized medical fields. Each setting presents unique challenges and opportunities for implementing empathetic care.

Primary Care

In primary care, providers often establish long-term relationships with patients, providing continuous and comprehensive care.

Empathy in this setting is crucial as it helps in understanding the broader context of a patient's health and life circumstances. Regular interactions provide multiple opportunities to build empathy and deeply understand patients' health behaviors and needs.

Hospital Care

In hospital settings, where care is often more fragmented, emphasizing empathy can significantly enhance the patient experience. Patients in hospitals are typically at a vulnerable point in their lives, and an empathetic approach can alleviate fears and anxieties about treatment and recovery. Training staff in empathy can ensure that patients feel supported and valued throughout their hospital stay.

Specialty Care

In specialty care, including fields such as oncology, psychiatry, or palliative care, empathy is particularly crucial. These areas often deal with complex emotional and physical issues, and an empathetic approach can make a significant difference in how patients cope with their conditions. Specialists must be skilled not only in their medical field but also in delivering care that acknowledges the emotional and psychological aspects of patient health.

Strategies for Enhancing Empathy in Healthcare

Developing and sustaining empathy in healthcare requires intentional strategies and practices that can be adopted at individual and institutional levels.

Training and Education

Incorporating empathy training into medical education can

prepare future healthcare professionals to better understand and integrate empathy into their practice. This training can include role-playing, patient interaction simulations, and reflective exercises that help learners understand the patient's perspective.

Patient Feedback Systems

Implementing systems to gather patient feedback can provide valuable insights into how patients perceive the care they receive and highlight areas where empathy might be lacking. This feedback can guide improvements and help healthcare providers focus on being more patient-centered.

Supporting Healthcare Providers

Providing support for healthcare providers is also essential, as dealing with patients' emotional and physical needs can be draining. Ensuring that healthcare workers have access to resources like counseling, peer support groups, and stress management training can help maintain their well-being and capacity for empathy.

Empathy is a critical element of patient-centered healthcare, fundamentally influencing the quality of care and patient outcomes. By fostering empathetic practices across all levels of healthcare, providers can create an environment where patients feel truly cared for and supported. This not only improves the effectiveness of medical treatments but also enriches the healthcare experience for patients and providers alike, creating a more compassionate and efficient healthcare system.

ϷϷϷ

"To empathize is to surrender the ego, to listen with
the heart, and to embrace the vulnerability of truly
seeing and being seen."

❥❥❥

NINETEEN
THE FUTURE OF EMPATHY: TRENDS AND PREDICTIONS

As we navigate deeper into the 21st century, the role of empathy in various domains of life—from personal relationships to global politics—is increasingly coming under the spotlight. Understanding the future trajectories of empathy involves examining current trends, technological advancements, and societal changes that are shaping how we understand and express this fundamental human capacity.

Technological Advancements and Empathy

Virtual Reality and Augmented Reality

One of the most significant technological advancements impacting empathy is the development of virtual reality (VR) and augmented reality (AR). These technologies offer unprecedented ways to experience the lives and perspectives of others. For example, VR has been used to simulate the experiences of refugees, the elderly, or even individuals suffering from specific medical conditions, allowing users to experience their challenges and hardships firsthand. This immersive technology could become a standard tool in education and professional training, enhancing empathy by providing deeper understanding and appreciation of diverse human experiences.

Artificial Intelligence and Machine Learning

Artificial intelligence (AI) and machine learning are also beginning to play roles in enhancing empathic interactions, albeit in more complex and sometimes controversial ways. AI systems can be trained to recognize human emotions through facial expressions, voice modulations, and other cues, potentially offering new ways to assess and respond to human feelings. However, this also raises ethical concerns about privacy, the authenticity of human interaction, and the potential manipulation of emotions.

Social and Cultural Trends

Globalization and Cultural Exchange

As globalization increases, so does the interaction between diverse cultures. This can lead to greater understanding and empathy across cultural boundaries, but it also presents challenges such as cultural homogenization and conflicts. The future of empathy will likely involve navigating these complex dynamics, striving to promote genuine intercultural understanding while respecting cultural identities.

Educational Shifts

There is a growing trend in education to prioritize social and emotional learning (SEL) alongside academic skills. SEL programs, which often include training in empathy, are designed to equip students with the emotional and social competencies needed to lead successful and compassionate lives. This trend is likely to expand, potentially leading to a generation that values and practices empathy more broadly than in the past.

Environmental and Global Health Challenges

Climate Change

As the impacts of climate change become more apparent, the need for empathy in addressing environmental issues is becoming critical. Empathy for future generations and people living in different parts of the world can drive the kind of cooperative and altruistic behavior needed to tackle global environmental challenges. Initiatives that humanize the effects of climate change and emphasize shared responsibility and fairness are likely to play crucial roles.

Pandemics and Global Health

The COVID-19 pandemic has highlighted the importance of empathy in managing global health crises. The future will likely see more emphasis on empathic leadership and policies in public health as a means to promote solidarity and compliance with health measures during pandemics.

Challenges to Empathy

Technology and Isolation

While technology offers tools to enhance empathy, it also poses challenges. The increased use of digital communication can lead to isolation and a decrease in face-to-face interactions, which are crucial for developing empathetic skills. The future of empathy will need to balance these technologies with real-world experiences that foster genuine human connections.

Political and Social Polarization

Increasing political and social polarization is another challenge for the future of empathy. Media echo chambers and ideological segregation can lead to reduced empathy for those with differing views. Addressing this issue may involve concerted efforts to promote media literacy, dialogue across divides, and education that emphasizes critical thinking and empathetic understanding.

Looking ahead, the future of empathy is intertwined with both challenges and opportunities. As we develop new technologies and expand our global interconnectedness, our capacity for empathy could either diminish or become a guiding principle for progress. By fostering environments that encourage empathetic development—from schools and workplaces to political and online arenas—we can ensure that empathy continues to evolve as a fundamental part of the human experience, enhancing how we interact with each other and address collective challenges in an increasingly complex world.

▷▷▷

"Empathy is the silent language of the soul—a universal dialect spoken by those who seek to understand, uplift, and connect with the humanity in us all."

♥♥♥

TWENTY

CULTIVATING PERSONAL EMPATHY: A STEP-BY-STEP GUIDE

Empathy is not just an innate trait but a skill that can be developed and enhanced over time. Cultivating personal empathy involves a series of deliberate practices and mindset shifts that can transform the way individuals interact with the world around them.

This comprehensive guide provides a step-by-step approach to developing deeper empathy, enriching personal relationships, enhancing professional interactions, and contributing positively to society.

Step 1: Self-Reflection and Awareness

Understanding Your Emotional Landscape

The journey to cultivating empathy begins with self-awareness. It is essential to understand your own emotions and triggers before you can empathize effectively with others. Regular self-reflection helps identify personal biases and preconceptions that may hinder empathetic interactions.

Journaling and Mindfulness

Practices such as journaling and mindfulness meditation are effective tools for developing self-awareness. Journaling can help you articulate feelings and reflect on your emotional responses to different situations. Mindfulness meditation, on the other hand, trains you to observe your thoughts and feelings without judgment, enhancing your ability to manage them more effectively.

Step 2: Educating Yourself About Others

Learning from Diverse Perspectives

Expanding your understanding of different cultures, life experiences, and perspectives is crucial for developing empathy. Engaging with books, films, and articles that explore diverse human experiences can open your eyes to the ways in which people's backgrounds shape their views and emotions.

Active Engagement with Different Communities

Where possible, actively engage with communities and groups outside of your immediate social circle.

This could involve participating in community events, volunteering with different organizations, or simply making an effort to build relationships with people who come from different backgrounds.

Step 3: Developing Active Listening Skills

Practicing Active Listening

Active listening is a core skill in empathetic engagement. It involves fully concentrating on the speaker, understanding their message, responding thoughtfully, and remembering the conversation.

This practice not only shows respect for the speaker but also provides deeper insight into their emotional state.

Workshops and Training

Consider participating in workshops or training programs focused on communication skills, particularly those that emphasize listening. These can provide practical tools and techniques for enhancing your ability to listen actively and respond empathetically.

Step 4: Empathy in Communication

Expressing Empathy in Conversations

When engaging in conversations, especially those involving emotional subjects, strive to express empathy verbally. Use phrases like "It sounds like you feel..." or "I can see why that would be upsetting," to demonstrate your understanding and concern.

Non-Verbal Communication

Remember that non-verbal cues, such as eye contact, nodding, and open body language, also play a critical role in showing empathy. Be mindful of your gestures and expressions, ensuring they convey your attention and care.

Step 5: Managing Emotional Boundaries

Recognizing Emotional Overload

While developing empathy is beneficial, it is also crucial to recognize when it becomes overwhelming. Learning to identify signs of emotional overload can help you maintain a healthy balance between connecting with others and preserving your own mental health.

Techniques for Emotional Regulation

Develop strategies for emotional regulation to prevent burnout. This could involve setting aside time for activities that help you recharge, such as hobbies, exercise, or spending time in nature.

Additionally, learning techniques such as deep breathing or progressive muscle relaxation can be effective in managing stress.

Step 6: Putting Empathy into Action

Volunteering and Community Service

One of the most impactful ways to exercise empathy is through volunteering and community service. These activities not only provide direct help to those in need but also deepen your understanding of the practical applications of empathy.

Advocacy and Support

Empathy can drive advocacy and support for causes that address human suffering or injustice. Whether it's through donating to a charity, supporting a social movement, or simply standing up for someone in need, your empathetic actions can have a significant impact.

Cultivating personal empathy is a rewarding process that enhances your interactions and contributes to a more compassionate society.

By following these steps and committing to continuous learning and practice, you can develop a profound empathetic capacity that will enrich both your life and the lives of those around you.

ϷϷϷ

"In a world hungering for connection, empathy is
the nourishment that sustains us, feeding the soul
with the warmth of understanding and the
sweetness of compassion."

❥❥❥

TWENTY-ONE
SUMMARY

This book explores the profound role of empathy in fostering a more compassionate and understanding world. Through a detailed examination across various spheres of life—interpersonal relationships, professional environments, education, healthcare, and global interactions—the chapters provide a comprehensive look at how empathy can transform interactions and promote a more inclusive society.

The Multidimensional Nature of Empathy

Empathy, as discussed in the initial chapters of this book, is not merely an emotional response but a complex, multidimensional skill that combines cognitive, emotional, and compassionate elements. It involves understanding another person's feelings and perspectives, sharing their emotional experiences, and being moved to help if needed. The ability to empathize influences not only personal relationships but also professional success and societal harmony.

Empathy in Personal and Professional Relationships

In personal relationships, empathy strengthens bonds by allowing individuals to understand and respond appropriately to the feelings and needs of others. In professional settings, especially in leadership and team dynamics, empathy contributes to more effective communication, collaboration, and workplace morale. Empathetic leaders are particularly adept at resolving conflicts, fostering team productivity, and ensuring employee satisfaction.

Educational and Healthcare Settings

The chapters dedicated to education and healthcare highlight empathy's critical role in these fields. In educational environments, fostering empathy among students not only enhances learning experiences but also prepares them for more harmonious social interactions. It instills a sense of social responsibility and helps in developing a generation that is more aware of and sensitive to the nuances of human emotions and cultural differences.

In healthcare, empathy significantly impacts patient care. Empathetic healthcare providers can achieve better patient outcomes, higher levels of patient satisfaction, and reduced rates of burnout among professionals. Patient-centered care, which is at the heart of empathetic practice in healthcare, emphasizes understanding the patient's experience and addressing their emotional and physical needs.

Global and Cultural Perspectives

Empathy extends beyond personal and immediate social interactions; it has a profound global dimension. Understanding and addressing cultural differences in expressing empathy are crucial for international relations and global cooperation. As societies become more interconnected, the ability to navigate and bridge cultural divides through empathy becomes more significant in solving global challenges such as climate change, international conflicts, and public health crises.

Challenges and Ethical Considerations

Empathy, while largely beneficial, is not without its challenges. The potential for empathic distress, where individuals become overwhelmed by the emotions of others, poses a significant risk, particularly in caregiving professions. Additionally, the ethical implications of empathy, such as biases in empathetic feelings towards certain groups or individuals, require careful consideration and management. This book addresses these challenges by offering strategies to maintain emotional health and balance empathy with objectivity and fairness.

Technological Influences

The role of technology in shaping empathy is another critical theme explored. While digital platforms can facilitate empathetic connections, they also present challenges, such as the risk of diminishing face-to-face interactions and the potential for misinterpreting emotional cues. Emerging technologies like virtual reality present new opportunities for empathy training by providing immersive experiences that can enhance understanding and compassion for others' experiences.

Moving Forward with Empathy

The final chapters of the book discuss how to cultivate and spread empathy effectively. Practical steps, including self-reflection, education, active listening, and community engagement, are detailed to help individuals enhance their empathetic abilities. The book emphasizes that empathy is a skill that can be learned and improved upon, suggesting that an investment in empathy education can yield substantial benefits for individuals and society alike.

In summary, this book posits that empathy is a cornerstone of compassionate living, essential for personal growth and societal progress. By embracing empathy, we can build stronger relationships, enhance professional environments, foster cultural understanding, and address global challenges more effectively. The journey toward cultivating a more empathetic society is complex and ongoing, but it is one of the most rewarding endeavors, promising a future where compassion and understanding reign supreme in our interactions and decisions.

ᗡᗡᗡ

Citation And References

This book represents the culmination of extensive research and meticulous analysis, incorporating a diverse range of sources, including numerous books, scholarly studies, and personal experiences. Additionally, I have scoured various websites to gather relevant information and data essential for the compilation of this work. I have taken every precaution to ensure the accuracy of the information presented and have diligently cited all sources to acknowledge their contributions.

Despite these efforts, the possibility of inadvertent errors remains. I deeply value the insights of my readers and appreciate any feedback that can help identify and rectify such inaccuracies. I encourage you to bring any discrepancies to my attention.

Your feedback is not only welcome but crucial, as it will aid in correcting current editions and enhancing the content of future ones. I am committed to maintaining the highest standards of accuracy and reliability in my work and thank you for your support and understanding.

Additionally, I firmly uphold the principle of freedom of speech and expression as guaranteed under Article 19(1)(a) of the Constitution of India, and I respect the diverse viewpoints and expressions of all readers.

ϷϷϷ

Other Books Of The Author

1. Empowering Minds: A Journey into Women's Self-Discovery and Power
2. The Dynamics of Motivation: Catalyzing Thought into Action
3. Meditation and Mental Well Being: The Path to Inner Peace and Clarity
4. The Psychology of Child Education: Nurturing Future Generations
5. Ethical Enlightenment: A Modern Guide to Living with Integrity
6. Voices of Empowerment: Stories of Women Rising Against Odds
7. Social Psychology in Everyday Life: Understanding Human Connections
8. The Essence of Motivational Speaking: Inspiring Change in Others
9. Balancing Acts: Women, Work, and the Will to Lead
10. Guiding with Grace: Raising Children with Compassion and Awareness
11. The Power of Positive Aging: Embracing Life After Fifty
12. Building Resilient Communities: Social Work in Action
13. The Ethical Educator: Principles for Teaching and Learning
14. From Insight to Impact: Social Psychology for a Better World
15. The Ethics of Empathy: A Guide to Ethical Living
16. The Science of Empowering the Self: Navigating Life's Challenges with Psychological Wisdom
17. The Mindful Conscious Leader: Meditation Techniques for Modern Management
18. Pioneering Spirit: Women's Pathways to Leadership and Empowerment
19. Feeling to Healing: The Role of Emotional Intelligence in Child Development
20. Transformative Talks and Words of Inspiration: Insights into Motivational Oratory

21. Green Ethics: A Path to Sustainable Living
22. Spiritual Integrity: Navigating Life with Moral Compassion
23. Clean Living, Clean Society: The Ethics of Cleanliness
24. Patriotic Spirits: Building a Nation on Positive Attitudes
25. Innovative Integrity & Vibrant Visions: The Ethical and Entrepreneurial Spirit of Gujarat
26. Youthful Visions, Endless Possibilities: Inspiring Ethics and Motivation in Children
27. Living Your Legacy: How to Motivate Others by Living Your Values
28. Secret of Healing Conversations: Ethical Practices in Counselling and Therapy
29. Creative Kindness: Crafting a Life of Compassion and Creativity
30. The Power of Appreciation: How Gratitude Can Transform Your Relationships
31. Bhagavad-Gita: Messages
32. Science of Art: The New Frontier of Fashion Modernism
33. Vivekananda's Virtues: A Blueprint for Modern Living
34. Empower Her: Navigating the Path to Women's Entrepreneurship
35. The Boundless Classroom: Innovations in Global Education
36. The Language of Leadership: Communicating with Authenticity and Impact
37. The Warrior's Mantra: Deciphering the Hanuman Chalisa
38. Echoes of Empathy: Transformative Stories of Social Service
39. Artful Living: Cultivating Creativity in Your Daily Routine
40. Finding Your Why: Discovering Your Passions and Charting Your Course
41. The Role of Social Media in Shaping Self-Esteem and Interpersonal Relationships among Adolescents

ɷɷɷ

Contact

Dr. Minakshi Bansal
Social Activist
Ahmedabad, Gujarat, Bharat
minakshiindiag20@yahoo.com

❦❦❦

|| LOKAHA SAMASTHAHA SUKHINO BHAVANTU ||

• 137 •

|| LOKAHA SAMASTHAHA SUKHINO BHAVANTU ||